CEJC

Walrus Migration

by Grace Hansen

Abdo
ANIMAL MIGRATION
Kids

abdopublishing.com

Published by Abdo Kids, a division of ABDO, P.O. Box 398166, Minneapolis, Minnesota 55439.

Copyright © 2018 by Abdo Consulting Group, Inc. International copyrights reserved in all countries. No part of this book may be reproduced in any form without written permission from the publisher.

Printed in the United States of America, North Mankato, Minnesota.

052017

092017

Photo Credits: iStock, National Geographic Creative, Shutterstock

Production Contributors: Teddy Borth, Jennie Forsberg, Grace Hansen

Design Contributors: Dorothy Toth, Laura Mitchell

Publisher's Cataloging in Publication Data

Names: Hansen, Grace, author.

Title: Walrus migration / by Grace Hansen.

Description: Minneapolis, Minnesota : Abdo Kids, 2018 | Series: Animal migration
    | Includes bibliographical references and index.

Identifiers: LCCN 2016962367 | ISBN 9781532100321 (lib. bdg.) |
    ISBN 9781532101014 (ebook) | ISBN 9781532101564 (Read-to-me ebook)

Subjects: LCSH: Walrus--Juvenile literature. | Walrus migration--Juvenile
    literature.

Classification: DDC 599.79--dc23

LC record available at http://lccn.loc.gov/2016962367

Table of Contents

Walruses

Walruses live in **shallow** waters in the Atlantic and Pacific oceans. Pacific walruses are much more **migratory** than Atlantic walruses. Pacific walruses travel up to 2,000 miles (3218.7 km) a year.

4

Pacific walruses can be found in the seas between Russia and Alaska.

Pacific walruses spend their winters in the Bering Sea. They sit huddled together on the **pack ice**. Walruses **mate** in the winter.

9

Following the Ice

As spring arrives, the pack ice begins to melt. The walruses head north where there will be more ice.

Walruses mostly travel by swimming. They sometimes ride on **ice floes**.

The Chukchi Sea is home for the summer. Females swim farther north than males. They find **pack ice**, **shallow** waters, and lots of food. They will give birth here.

Baby walruses are born in May or June. Mothers care for their young. They feed and protect them.

Back to the Bering Sea

As fall arrives, the walruses prepare to move south again. Males, females, and young walruses reunite in the Bering Sea.

Walruses huddle closely on the **pack ice** to keep warm. They **mate**, eat, and wait for spring to arrive once again.

Walrus Migration Routes

22

Summer Home   Winter Home   **Breeding Area**

Glossary

ice floe – a large, flat area of ice floating in the ocean.

mate – come together for breeding.

migratory – moving from one place to another at different times of the year.

pack ice – a very large sheet of ice floating in the sea that is made from smaller pieces that have frozen together.

shallow – not deep.

Index

abdokids.com

Use this code to log on to abdokids.com and access crafts, games, videos and more!

Abdo Kids Code:
AWK0321